The Art of the Chase

The Art of the Chase

Because Dating's Not a Science—It's an Art

Hayley DiMarco
and Michael DiMarco

Revell
Grand Rapids, Michigan

© 2007 by Hungry Planet

Published by Fleming H. Revell
a division of Baker Publishing Group
P.O. Box 6287, Grand Rapids, MI 49516-6287

Printed in the United States of America

Library of Congress Cataloging-in-Publication Data
DiMarco, Hayley.
    The art of the chase / Hayley DiMarco and Michael
DiMarco.
        p.   cm. — (A marriable book)
    ISBN 10: 0-8007-3149-2 (pbk.)
    ISBN 978-0-8007-3149-6 (pbk.)
    1. Man-woman relationships. 2. Dating (Social
customs) 3. Mate selection. I. DiMarco, Michael. II.
Title.
HQ801.D5625 2007
646.7'7—dc22
                                                        2006031266

Excerpts from **Marriable: Taking the Desperate Out of Dating**

Published in association with Yates & Yates, LLP, Literary Agents,
Orange, California.

THE
MARRIABLE
GALLERY

talk

# of Modern
Chasing
Art

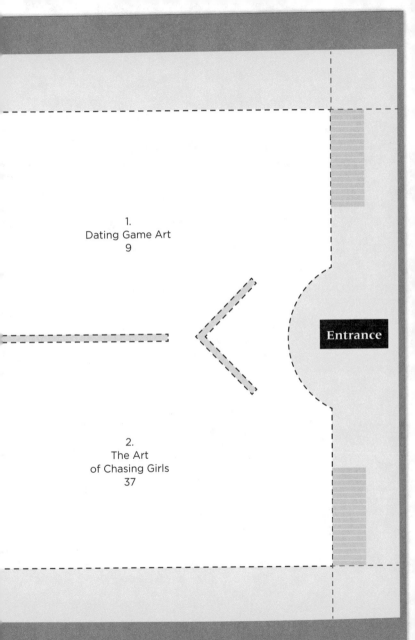

Entrance

Dating Game
Art

1

Have you ever felt like giving up on dating? You like someone, you think they like you, but you just can't get things rolling? Are you frustrated that your soul mate still hasn't come knocking at your door? Would it help to know that there is an art to this fumbling around blind activity we call dating? Well, have no fear, help is here! (Trite, we know.) Whether you call dating a dance or a game, knowing your role and the rules of the game or standards for the dance will go a long way in helping you find the person you're looking for. Not only that, but realizing that "finding the one" is a series of actions and reactions instead of an act of patience is the first step in embracing the Art of the Chase.

From the dawn of man, we see the chase. Cat and mouse. Games of tag and dodgeball. Jeff Gordon and Dale Earnhardt Jr. That's what dating and NASCAR have in common—both have you going in circles—but only NASCAR races guarantee a finish line! And what typically is happening in singles circles today is good men and women not knowing how fast to drive,

10

which direction to start, and who's to set the pace for the race when some singles won't even climb into their cars and others know no other speed than "pedal to the metal."

In this book, we hope to help you find your way in the dating world, with a clear purpose that doesn't have you spinning your wheels with no end in sight and nothing to show for it. We hope this little tome, much like our books *Marriable: Taking the Desperate Out of Dating* and the other *Art Of* books, will be practical, humorous, useful, and utterly relevant to learning the Art of the Chase.

Some singles just pretend to be in the race.

The Dating Game

When we tell people to look at dating like a game, some get really offended, as if we just told them to be someone they're not or to purposely go out and break hearts in order to win a game. But the fact that dating is a game doesn't mean it's a cruel thing used for malicious or even entertainment purposes. What we mean is that just like the games you loved to play when you were a kid, a good dating game requires a plan and a strategy for success. Every time you play Battleship or Stratego, you need to have a plan if you want to ultimately win. Dating is the same way, only in dating the goal of the game is not to capture a flag or sink a battleship but to find the person of your dreams and live happily ever after. In every aspect of our lives, from board games to career moves, we have plans and strategies for getting what we want. So why should all that be considered a deceitful ploy when it comes to dating? The truth is that whether you admit it or not, every time you date, you are playing the dating game. In other words, you have game pieces (you), an opponent (fear, loneliness, etc.), and something you want to ultimately win (a heart).

All we ask is that you take any negative connotations of game playing and throw them out the window. We are talking not about playing games with people's minds or hearts but about playing the game of love and loving it. The dating game is not a game of emotional sniping but a game of attraction and pursuit. See, when you can start to think of dating or anything else as a game, you can get a clearer picture in your head of what you are doing and how to do it, because with games there are rules, strate-

The dating game
is not a game of
emotional sniping but
a game of attraction
and pursuit, like a
good game of tag.

Dating Game Art

gies, and goals. We hope that when you play the game of dating like you'll read about here in *The Art of the Chase*, you can start to let go of some of the dysfunctional and emotional decisions you've made in the past when it comes to love and start to make some smart, educated, and tactical decisions to help you on your way to finding true love. It's like we always say: If you keep doing what you're doing, you'll keep getting what you've got. And the question is, is that enough?

If your answer is no, then congratulations! You're ready to move on to master the Art of the Chase. And when you do, you might just be surprised how much easier the entire dating game is than you once thought it was.

If you're sick of all the mind games, then you've come to the right place. We are suggesting not that dating is a mind game but that dating with purpose and strategy will get you a lot farther than you've gotten up to now. The dating game can be the best game both you and your date have ever played if you will read and implement *The Art of the Chase*.

"I hate people who play games with your head. They're such jerks!"

"I don't know about you, but I'm sick of all the games!"

"I don't want to play any games with you. I just want to be real."

Men Chase, Women Catch

It might be an old-fashioned notion in some circles, but we believe that the true Art of the Chase dictates that man chases woman and woman catches man. But how does that happen? Or better yet, why? Let's start with the latter. Why should men be the ones doing the chasing? Surely a woman can do anything a man can do. Yes, that's true. We wouldn't argue with that. But just because you **can** do something doesn't mean you **should**! And the same is true of chasing. Women can chase men all day long. But the question is, do women really want men who are too afraid to chase them? Do women really want to be the stronger person, the emotional rock of the relationship? Do you, as a woman, really want to be with a man who wasn't attracted to you enough to go after you himself?

Here's the truth that you have to realize if you're a woman who thinks that chasing is up to whoever wants to do it: When a man is attracted to a woman, he will chase her. It's in his DNA. If he doesn't chase her, that's because he isn't interested (or never learned how to chase!). Period. The end. So when you find a man and he's not moving, don't assume he's just waiting for you to make the first move. Sure, he might respond well when you do, but that's because he's flattered. Who wouldn't be? But it's not because you're the woman of his dreams. It's not because he can't live without you. And it's not because you're all he thinks about. It's because you're a woman and you made it easy. And men are lazy creatures.

The scepter of manhood!

> **Exhibit A:** the remote control, their favorite household item.
>
> **Exhibit B:** the dirty dishes in the sink of every bachelor in town.
>
> **Exhibit C:** the built-in mini-fridge in the armchair.

Need we go on? If there is an easy way to do things, man will figure it out! So when you, the woman, do the asking, he easily says yes because what the heck, all the work's already been done. Wow, what an expression of devotion! What a testimony to his passion for you. Wrong! But hey, you'll do until he finds someone who turns him on enough for him to want to chase her.

When a man is attracted to something, be it a car, a job, or a woman, he will stop at nothing to get it. Just look at every teenage guy who spends every last penny to buy a PlayStation or

17

new rims for his car. He'll go to school, work three jobs, and save up every penny in order to have the car his heart yearns for! Because when a man really wants something, nothing will stop him from going after it. This is why we say men chase! If they don't, then frankly, they aren't that interested. And we want women to spend their time and energy on men who are interested, not men who think, "She'll do." How romantic! So if you want the Art of the Chase to change your love life, you're going to have to concur, or at least give a listen to the idea that men pursue and women catch.

We say women catch because ultimately women do play a huge role in attracting the men whose hearts they capture. But it's a subtle, mysterious, and beautiful role, not a direct, "I don't have a lot of time, my biological clock is ticking, let's get this show on the road" kind of role. When women decide that it's up to them to chase a man, they end up in one of two scenarios: Either they look desperate or they look unremarkable. If he's not at all interested, she looks desperate, and if he is mildly interested, then she comes off looking rather unremarkable. Take it from our favorite commentary on the dating lives of singles today, TV's **The Bachelor.** Remember the bachelorette who told the bachelor upon their first meeting, "I need to procreate!

Are you ready to procreate?" Millions of jaws dropped in disbelief all across America. Why? She was only being assertive and honest, two very healthy qualities, right? Okay, we'll give you that, but what did those healthy qualities get her? The boot!

Just because you **can** do something doesn't mean you **should.** If you watch carefully, you'll notice that every season, the bachelorette who pesters and paws after the bachelor never makes it very far. Meanwhile, the one who lets him chase her in the midst of all those girls, the one who lets him do the work, is always one of the final three. And most of the time the bachelor will remark how mysterious she is, whereas those who say things like, "What are you doing with the other bachelorettes?" "Why do you even like **her**?" or "I need to know how you feel" soon find themselves roseless and on their way home. The Art of the Chase plays itself out each season that the bachelorettes line up to capture the newest bachelor. When women chase, they look desperate, but when they let men chase them, they look desirable.

If this seems preposterous and outdated to you, we'll ask the question again: *If you keep doing what you're doing, you'll keep getting what you're getting—is that enough?*

Tag! You're It!

When you were little, didn't you just love a wild game of tag? Remember running around the yard or neighborhood chasing after anyone you could find to tag in order to win the game? Just thinking about it can make your mind and heart race. Ah, the good old days when playing with others was as simple as counting to ten and then running after them with your arms stretched out in front of you. Screams of excitement filled the air, and joy was in vast supply. But can you imagine starting a game of tag with friends, counting to ten, and then opening your eyes to find them all standing right in front of you? You think it must be a trick, so you reach out to touch one of them, sure they will run as soon as you move, but they just stand there smiling. You touch them and yell, "Tag! You're it!" and they just stand there smiling. What a boring game of tag that would be. Where's the running? Where's the hot pursuit? What's the point without the chasing?

The Art of the Chase asks that same question about dating. What's the point of dating without the chase? *Attraction* and *pursuit* are the watchwords of the dating game. They are the reasons and the equipment used to find and capture the heart of the one we love. So what has happened to the Art of the Chase? In **Marriable** we talked about the complaint of so many women that men just aren't asking them out. They bemoan the fact that guys are playing it safe and not risking anything in any kind of pursuit. Why is this such a common complaint? Are men really not asking as much as they used to? Or is it that like in our boring game of tag, the women aren't playing the game as it should be played? Either way, chasing and pursuing seems to be a relic of the past. In the old days women were pursued and men weren't afraid to do that pursuing. They saw it as their duty, their role in the dating game. But today things seem to have gotten all topsy-turvy. Men, in an attempt to respect the feelings of women and their right to be independent and equal, have backed off of the pursuit and opted for friendliness. Hence the epidemic of couples who are "just friends" but where one or both finds they want so much more but are too afraid to ask.

Are you suggesting I have to *get up* to do this pursuing?

Dating Game Art

Being Just Friends Is a Waste of Time

We can't say it any more plainly than this: If one of you doesn't have chemistry, you don't have chemistry as a couple. One of the dangers with male/female friendships is that more often than not, one of the two wants something more from the relationship. In the end, usually either a heart is broken or, at the very least, the person with the crush is wasting time not looking elsewhere. If you are holding on to a long-term friendship in hopes that one day it will magically turn to love, you are lying to yourself. The chances that your friend will wake up one day and see you in a totally different and romantic light are miniscule. Save yourself the heartache. Keep friendship with the same sex and **save the opposite sex for love.**

from *Marriable: Taking the Desperate Out of Dating*

When you create an environment where men feel like sharks if they pursue women and where women feel like they can and should do everything for themselves, you end up with a generation of singles "waiting" longer and longer to get married. You end up single and hating it! Sure, you're happy being single. You love coming home to your cat and your TV every night. You don't need anyone else to be happy. Right! We feel your pain. The truth is, we were both thirty-seven and single and hating it. Sure, our lives were fulfilling. We both loved our jobs, our friends, our families, and even our pets, but there was something missing—or rather, someone. We weren't lame or dysfunctional because we wanted a partner. And neither are you. If you picked up this book, it's probably because you are like us; you just want to love and be loved. And there's nothing wrong with that. Now wouldn't you like the opportunity to look for that special someone in a more efficient way than the way you've been doing it? If so, then give the following pages a try. We believe that if men are allowed to chase women and women are allowed to feel desirable and wanted, then things will get much, much better for all of them. *The Art of the Chase* was created in order to help men and women better understand the beauty of the chase and the excitement of the catch. So let's see if we can't take this world and shake it up, and what we hope we will find is an amazing new adventure with your "pot of gold" at the end of the rainbow.

The Anatomy of the Chase

to chase: to follow regularly or persistently with the intention of attracting or alluring

Being chased is fun. Whether it's in the yard, in the pool, or around the house, being chased can be a lot of fun. And it's no different for women. When they are being chased by someone they like, they are having the time of their lives. Being chased by a man means he finds you irresistible. It means that you are attractive to him and he just can't keep away. Being chased makes a woman feel like a woman—alluring, feminine, wanted. If you're a woman and it's never happened to you, we're sorry. It should. And we hope it will. But before all you men run out and start chasing random women around, let's explore a bit of the anatomy of the chase.

Chasing someone, as we define it, is a mutual desire. If one or the other isn't interested, then this isn't the Art of the Chase. No man wants to chase a woman who doesn't want him, or at least no sane man wants to chase someone who doesn't want to be caught. And no woman wants to be chased by someone she doesn't want to be captured by. But how do you know if the desire is mutual? Do you just come out and ask them? No. That would ruin the chase. The anatomy of the chase starts at the beginning. But of course! And the beginning is flirting.

Often referred to as the "chasing bones," the legs are not even necessarily required for a good "chase."

Hide-and-Seek: The Official Rules

Hide-and-seek is best played in an area with lots of hiding spots, like a forest or a large house. The game starts with all players in one spot. The person who is "it" covers his eyes while he counts out loud for a predetermined number of seconds, often with the aid of a word that takes about one second to say (e.g., "one alligator, two alligator . . ." or "one Mississippi, two Mississippi . . ."). Meanwhile, the other players hide. "It" announces when he has finished counting by shouting a phrase such as "Ready or not, here I come!" Then he tries to find the hiding players. The next "it" is either the first or the last player found, depending on the rules agreed to by the players.

Players may move to other hiding spots while "it" isn't look-ing. *Those who can remain hidden the longest are considered the best players.*

The Art of Flirting

to flirt: to make playfully romantic or sexual overtures

The best way to find out if someone is interested in you is to flirt. Flirting has gotten a bad rap in a lot of circles. Tagged as malicious or manipulative, flirting has often been misunderstood. The truth is that flirting can be used for selfish and destructive reasons, but that's only done by stupid people. If you truly care about the opposite sex and understand the power of flirtation, you should be able to handle and even enjoy the Art of Flirting, and so should be the objects of your flirtation. The beautiful thing about flirting in the hands of a smart person is that it can help alleviate fears, insecurities, and discouragement when facing potential dates. It's like an advance warning system that allows you to send in a recon team to figure out the lay of the land before deciding whether or not to advance your troops. And it's the best way to discover a connection without being slapped, laughed at, or overlooked. Flirting is a kind of subtle communication between two people that allows them to explore the possibility of chemistry.

One of the big reasons flirting gets a bad rap is because people who aren't interested in pursuing a relationship or are already *in* a relationship with someone else use it purely as amusement. When you have no intention of starting something with someone but flirt with them anyway, you run the risk of leading them on, and that can lead to a lot of embarrassment and hurt feelings. So the flirting we are talking about in *The Art of the Chase* is the good, healthy kind that is meant to show another available single that you are interested in testing the waters to see if there is any mutual attraction.

Nonverbal Flirting

Nonverbal signals are really the very beginning of the whole thing. Nonverbal flirting before a conversation gives the object of your flirting the green light to approach you.

Top 7 Ways We Flirt without Saying a Word

The second (and third, and fourth . . .) glance. When you are interested in someone, you tend to continue to track them from across the room. If you find them attractive, you can't help but want to look at them. And it's that attraction and your subsequent tracking of them that is a sign that you are interested in talking with them.

Sweet smile. You've seen it before: that subtle smile that says so much. It's the flirting smile, and it looks different than other smiles, but only in subtle ways. You'll know it when you see it. A smile from a stranger along with a few more of these nonverbals is a good sign that the next step of verbal flirting can take place. But women need to be careful with their smiles. Sometimes men have a hard time distinguishing a friendly smile from a flirting one. So men, if you aren't sure about her smile, wait for some other signals before you dive in on an unintentional flirt.

IT'S NOT A
TUBER !
(It's a flirty
po-tah-to.)

Drawing attention. When someone is interested in you, they tend to go out of their way to get your attention. You know you've done it before. When you see a hottie across the room, you suddenly have to go to the bathroom, taking a path that takes you right past their table. Coincidence? I don't think so! Putting yourself

Dating Game Art

in the sight line of your crush is a good way to flirt without putting your heart on the line.

Hair play. This is exclusively a female technique (we hope!). When a girl is interested in a guy, something in her just makes her want to play with her hair. It's almost subconscious. And guys notice. If you are interested in a guy and aren't the hair-playing type, you might want to give it a try anyway. It sends a clear signal to a guy that you are interested in him.

Soft touch. Another almost subconscious form of flirting is the soft touch. When you are talking with someone and you agree with them and like them, you tend to want to touch them on the arm or the leg. This sends a huge signal that you are interested without coming right out and saying it. The touch isn't prolonged, and it definitely isn't gropey. It's just a quick connection that says, "I want more." The touch of agreement lightly placed on the arm helps you both to decide if there is chemistry.

Eye contact. Here's the thing: If someone *isn't* interested in you, then they probably aren't going to make a ton of eye contact. That's one of the great things about understanding flirting. When you do, you can save yourself a ton of grief just by watching the signals you are getting and sending the right signals yourself. So if you like someone, be sure you spend enough time looking them in the eye. For girls, giving the subtle look and then looking down quickly is a great sign of attraction as well.

Body language. If you want to flirt with someone without using words, then use your body. Mimic the positioning of the other person's body by crossing your arms if theirs are crossed or leaning in when they lean in. It's actually another one of those subconscious things that we tend to do when we agree with someone—we hold our bodies in the same way as theirs. So if you like someone, pay attention to how they are sitting and show them that you agree.

Be careful about taking mimicking too far.

After that initial impression has been sent and received, it's time to move to the verbal part of flirting. The most exciting part of flirting can be the verbal sparring—sending ideas back and forth at each other like a rapid game of volleyball. Each phrase piques the interest of the other person and spurs them on to return another interesting or witty remark. The verbal part of flirting is really what helps you to establish some common ground that will give you a solid idea about compatibility before you move on to the asking out part.

Bump, set, flirt.

Unfortunately, not everyone is as quick on their feet as they'd like to be when it comes to bantering with the opposite sex. That doesn't mean you shouldn't give it a try. It probably just means you haven't found the right person. Flirting is amazing because it can help two people who have struck out time and again in the charm department suddenly light up when the right person crosses their path. If you are able to flirt well with anyone, then you might never know if you've found the right one. But if you strike out more often than not, then take heart, because when the banter is good, you'll have a sure sign that this person would be a good one to pursue further. But just in case you aren't willing to flirt and fail a hundred more times before you find your flirting match, here are some tips for the tongue-tied.

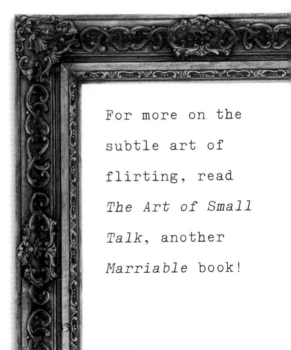

For more on the subtle art of flirting, read *The Art of Small Talk*, another *Marriable* book!

Be Confident. People often say that confidence is attractive. But good-looking, successful people aren't the only ones who can be confident. Confidence is something you can choose to exhibit regardless of how you feel about yourself. And one of the best ways to appear confident is with the use of small talk. People who are willing to talk with strangers or familiar strangers appear very confident to those around them. So the first thing to consider before you write off flirting with the opposite sex forever is changing your confidence level by increasing your prowess in the Art of Small Talk. The way you speak and the words you use, as well as the nonverbal signals you give off, all add to your confidence factor. And you will notice that none of this has to do with how you look or how much money you make. Confidence can be manufactured with a little research and hard work.

Use Humor. You don't have to be a comedian to use humor to flirt with someone. The key is to remember (1) not to take yourself too seriously and (2) not to take your crush too seriously. When you worry too much about how you look or what you're going to say, you come across as stiff and unapproachable. People who are comfortable and not afraid to look stupid find humor much easier to come by. Using yourself as the subject of your jokes can often be

34

endearing. A lot of people use self-deprecating humor in mild doses and have great success. But don't go overboard with this or you'll sound like you're just looking for sympathy or something. Remember, confidence is attractive, so if you're confident enough to laugh at yourself, you will set your crush at ease and help them to understand that you're a charming companion.

One word of warning: Stay away from sarcasm unless it's self-deprecating. Sarcasm can come off as negative, bitter, or superior and can instantly cool off any heat that had been generated. Keep your witticisms lighthearted and positive and you're likely to attract a positive person.

Stay away from this as well. It's just kinda gross.

Take a cue from your childhood and don't take your crush too seriously. Remember the old days on the playground when you liked someone? What did you do but run up to them and hit them, of course! Picking on someone we like is as natural as a peacock spreading its feathers to catch a mate. It might seem like child's play, but that's what's so fun about it. A little playful picking on can be a sure sign that the chemistry set is boiling over. But be careful with this approach; overdo it and you'll come across like a real jerk. But using it in small doses sends a strong signal that you want more of what you see.

Listen. When it comes to chasing or catching someone, listening is of utmost importance. It's all well and good to be funny and confident, but if you aren't willing to shut up and listen to your date or potential date, you'll be dropped like a hot potato. This one seems like a no-brainer, but that doesn't make it easy to do. Practice listening to everyone you meet and know so that when you finally find the one you want to date, listening will be second nature.

Flirting really is a give-and-take situation. The best flirt is someone who takes on their fair share of the job of flirting but gives you permission to play your equal part. It's a 50/50 thing. Whether you are ready to chase a woman or catch a man, taking a central role in the Art of Flirting is part of your job. If you still feel weak in this department, then do your research. Check out *The Art of Small Talk* and maybe even *The Art of Rejection*. Be willing to learn and grow, and you'll then be ready to move on to the rest of *The Art of the Chase.*

The Art
of Chasing Girls

2

Taking Charge

Okay, this chapter is for all the guys out there. But we aren't kidding ourselves—we know you women will want to read it just as much if not more. And we hope you'll be cheering us on as you read our plans for helping men get a little more assertive on the dating scene.

We said it earlier, but it's worth repeating: Men chase and women catch. It's natural for a guy to go after what he wants; it just seems like guys don't want much more than their Xbox controller and a plate of nachos. But surely that isn't the case. We know you guys want to ask girls out, you want to be charming and assertive and manly, but you just aren't sure how to do it or how she'll react. Trust us when we say that if you do it right, she'll love it. Even if she's got a feminist streak in her and insists she can do it all herself, she still will be flattered and charmed by a man who knows how to be a man—and by that we mean he knows what he wants and how to go after it.

38

Women of all sociological bents can find comfort in a man who knows what he's doing and, better yet, in a man who finds her so alluring that he will do whatever it takes to show her his affection. In a world where guys and girls are often friends, it's time to step out of the herd and make some noise if you want to be noticed as more than a "girlfriend." Just as an exercise, let's compare women to a herd of beautiful and graceful gazelles. If you walk into the herd and all the gazelle girls look up from their lunch of fresh green grass, smile, and then go back to eating, the Art of the Chase has somehow eluded you. In order for the chase to take place, you must be seen not as just another gazelle but as something different. Something that can get their blood flowing and their hearts racing. The Art of the Chase requires men who are tired of being "one of the gazelles" and want to stir things up like a wild lion by taking charge of the dating relationship.

Fairy tales color girlhood dreams of love and romance from the day girls first hear, "Once upon a time." Something about the fairy tale of love and romance clicks within the heart of a woman. It's never a tale of a princess who rescues her prince from a terrible spell placed on him by the witch. It isn't about the girl who searches out the sweet man who left one of his glass Hush Puppies behind after a wonderful night at the ball. Those kinds of fairy tales would leave girls bewildered and uninterested in more. It just doesn't click with the average girl's heart to want to chase after or rescue a boy. It's just the opposite. So why would we think that as grown-ups we'd be any different? Why have some women and men bought the lie that women can do the chasing and the saving and things will still turn out as sweet? It really goes against every fiber of our beings to flip the roles of prince and princess, of lover and beloved.

No, a man who takes charge and sweeps her off her feet, that's the stuff a girl's heart dreams of. Women have taken matters into their own hands because they have felt powerless to attract men any other way, but you can change things by deciding to become the kind of man that takes charge, stands up, and acts like a man!

We want to give you, the man, permission to take back your role as chaser, protector, and provider. We want to tell you that even if some women out there have abandoned so-called traditional roles, still more yearn for the old days when men were men and women were treated like women. So if that's the kind of woman you are interested in, it's time to get to work on the Art of the Chase so that you can step up and take back the role of manhood!

Meeting Women

It's time to stop complaining about not being able to meet women and start doing something about it. The truth is that there are just as many women bemoaning the difficulty of tracking down men as there are men. Now all we have to do is get you two together. Let's say you just bought a new Xbox 360 and you're wondering what games you can play on it. What's the first thing you do? A little research, maybe? Get online and look up which games are available now and which are upcoming releases? Find out which old Xbox games are backward compatible with the new unit? Maybe talk to some friends? You get the picture: You get to work. You find out what you need to find out in order to get what you want. Then what? Do you just sit on the couch and stare at the incredible opening graphics on the console but never hit start because you have no games? Or maybe you get in the car, go to where the games are, and shop for the perfect one. Of course, they're expensive, so you can't just run in and buy them all; you

Remember when love was simple, like a joystick with one button?

have to be deliberate. You use your wealth of knowledge and pick wisely.

Think of meeting women like finding the perfect video game. First of all, it requires a little research. What kind of women are you compatible with? Athletic women? Artsy women? Techie women? Once you think you know that, then it's time to figure out where those women are and to make a plan to go out looking for them.

No More Mr. Nice Guy

If you think the whole "looking for women" thing just sounds too shark-like, then you might be suffering from nice guy syndrome. You don't want to be the creep who shows up at a singles group scanning the crowd for his next kill. And women appreciate that. But don't let the shark guy ruin it for everyone else. Being a nice guy doesn't mean you don't *chase* women. It just means that you only chase women who are showing signs of interest. Remember the whole thing about flirting? Now that you know how that part of the game works, you know if you're being asked to play or not. Men have the responsibility to "challenge" women to a date, and women have the responsibility to accept or decline the challenge. So no more Mr. Nice Guy, no more feeling like it is offensive to pursue women, because it isn't. It's essential. Sure, solitaire is a game too, but you need a challenger to start playing hearts.

43

What Women Love

The world holds all kinds of women and all kinds of things that they want. Granted, it's hard to generalize on the subject, because they are all so different, but one thing rings true no matter who the woman: They love romance. Romance is a very common feminine trait, but if you want to get the girl, you're more than likely going to have to get the art of it. Most women love romance and find it an integral part of the dating process. And it's no wonder, since they've been practicing it over and over again in their imaginations since they were little girls. Just like you've been imagining the perfect car since you could say "***vroom vroom***," women have been imagining the perfect romance since they put on their first tiara, princess dress, and pair of Mom's high heels.

The world has done men a disservice by playing on this deep desire of women and giving them perfect romance in the form of the chick flick. Now this is what most women measure your efforts by. Although we don't think that's fair, it's kind of the state of affairs. If she's seen it on the big screen, then she's dreamt that one day it will happen to her. But the good news is that you can use that to your advantage—the chick flick, that is. If you want to romance

44

a woman but feel like you are lacking in that department, just watch a few chick flicks, and soon you'll get the swing of things.

But first this **Romantic Warning**: One of the definitions of *romance* in Webster's dictionary is something that "lacks basis in fact." And that seems like a pretty good definition. Romance is temporary. It isn't a way of life. But when women are dating someone, they can often live with the illusion that the dreamy romance of today will be the dreamy romance of the rest of the relationship, and that just can't happen. We know you guys are working hard just to conjure up enough romance to win her heart. It would be agony to keep it up 24/7 like a never-ending chick flick. The reality is that life has its romantic moments and its mundane ones, and both have value. The trouble comes when women let their hearts rule their minds and start to believe that the romantic feelings they have translate into eternal love. That's not always the case. You can have romance without love. So the warning for you, the man, is to be kind and not use romance to lead a woman on. Know that the romantic

Even knights don't keep their armor on 24/7, which means most of the time they will just be "normal."

moments you share have a powerful impact on her heart and cause her to see things differently than in her saner moments. Nothing is wrong with romance as long as both of you understand that it's going to ebb and flow and that it most certainly doesn't equal love. ***Love is a decision, not a feeling.*** That was said for the women reading this! Don't let the romance convince you of anything.

That said, we really think that being super romantic in a new relationship can be as dangerous as being sexual. The reason is that romance is as much a turn-on to a woman as sex is to you. And when she gets turned on, she starts to lie to herself about you. How much she loves you, how perfect you are, etc. A girl will think she's in love, and then if and when you break up, you will break her heart. And other girls, the crazy ones who lie to themselves as well, are sure this most definitely is love and you most definitely are the one. These are the women who go psycho on you and won't let you break up with them. They threaten suicide, physical pain, or damage to your personal belongings. So beware the use of romance. It is a powerful tool, but it can backfire on you if you aren't using it wisely!

Let us just say again that using romance as a tool to get what you want from someone you know you aren't interested in is the slimiest of slimy. We want you to learn what women want so when you find someone you care about, you can care for her by meeting her needs, or shall we say **desires**. No, romance is not a need. Air is, water is, but not romance, yet it is still the heart cry of most women.

Chick Flicks—aka Female Porn

Pornography is defined by Webster's as "the depiction of acts in a sensational manner so as to arouse a quick intense emotional reaction." And it isn't just for men! Chick flicks and romance novels give women very strong emotional reactions, even to the point of tears on occasion. What they offer to women is exactly what they crave: the perfect man, who unfortunately doesn't exist. He's a man who never farts, burps, or talks rudely. He's always in love with her, he's always dreaming of her, he always **gets** her and is the answer to all her problems. In other words, he doesn't exist. Female porn does to women exactly what sexual porn does to men: It turns them on, gets them hot and

The perfect man.

bothered, and then leaves them with nothing but a warped sense of the opposite sex.

Female porn sells them a lie about how a man should look and act. The fantasy created by female porn can put men at a disadvantage and leave single women feeling more lonely and incomplete than ever when the guy from the movie never shows up at their door.

Even though we spend a lot of time talking to women about this very subject, we aren't deluding ourselves into thinking that chick flicks will die a sudden death because women will wake up and stop feeding their appetites for romance. It won't happen. So when the world gives you lemons, make lemonade, we always say. Translation: Men might as well use chick flicks to their advantage and research their way into the hearts of women. Think of them as your Romance 101 class. If you can stomach it, you'll have to watch a few until you get the idea. But female porn offers a great deal of insight into what women want.

Okay, now back to our regularly scheduled chick flick class.

The cute meeting. In the best romance movies, the couple usually meets in some kind of cute way. Usually the guy does something that girls think is cute and sweet, and it gets the attention of the girl. This isn't always the easiest thing to do, but if you spend some time thinking about it, you might be able to come up with some cute ways to express your interest. Cute always captures the hearts of women. That's why you'll see it so many times in chick flicks. Whether you are ice skating and you bump into each other and fall down in each other's arms or your dog wraps its leash around her legs, a serendipity kind of meeting is very attractive to women.

Just make sure I have a really long leash if you want me to go wrapping around anyone's legs.

Something keeps them apart. In most chick flicks, about two-thirds of the way through the movie, something looks like it will keep the couple apart. Be it a misunderstanding or a fight or a third party who wants the relationship destroyed, there is always some stumbling block to true love. This leads to the anticipation and that sense of excitement that comes when you aren't sure if what you want to happen will happen or not. Although we don't suggest playing with a woman's emotions by pretending to leave her or lose her, you can simulate this very emotion in some romantic ways.

1. ***Don't appear desperate.*** Don't call her fifteen times a day to find out what she's doing. There's no excitement or wonder in that. Have a life. Be a little bit mysterious. Don't go out with another woman to make her jealous, but do spend time with friends. Don't spend all your time with her when you first meet.

2. ***Don't share all your emotions.*** We've talked about this at length in our books ***The Art of Small Talk*** and ***Marriable***, but we just want to reiterate. Don't overshare. When you do, you look more like a girlfriend than a potential guy friend. The strong silent type leaves women wondering, "Does he or doesn't he?"

3. ***Don't go too fast.*** When you go too fast emotionally or physically, you lose that sense of anticipation.

4. ***Don't always be available.*** Something worth having is rare and valuable. If you're always free whenever she asks if you're available, it might seem like you're waiting around for her. Have a life!

50

The dance. Dancing is such an amazing thing for women that a whole subgenre of chick flicks revolves solely around dancing. If you can't dance, maybe you could sign up for a dance class. You might even meet someone there, but at the very least you'll make yourself much more *Marriable*. Women find nothing more romantic than a man who will dance with them!

So sign up for a ballroom class or go in for salsa lessons at the local salsa club. It would even be fun to invite a girl you're interested in to take her with you. That way you get to dance with her every week, and she'll love it!

The ultimate grand gesture. In chick flicks, by the end of the film the hero usually makes some kind of grand gesture that affirms to the woman that he truly is the one and he would do anything for her. This isn't the kind of inappropriate grand gesture we've talked about in other books (see *The Art of the First Date* and *Marriable*), like two dozen red roses on your second date. It's a real affirmation of devotion and love, but it can't come too early or it will mess up everything. So be sure that if you copy any of the grand gestures you see in a chick flick, you save it until you are completely sure that all she wants from you is your undying love. If you pull the trigger too early,

51

you'll lose that sense of anticipation that is so key in the art of romance, and you just might scare her off.

In truth, the ultimate grand gesture is a ring with a proposal, and like any grand gesture, you need to know someone well before pulling the trigger.

Chick Flick No-No's
"I hate you so much I love you!"

Chick flicks can give you a good idea of what women find romantic, but they can also teach you some bad habits. Many a romantic comedy starts with a couple that does nothing but fight when they meet. They can't stand each other, but the audience can still sense the chemistry. Of course, by the end of two hours, they've figured out that they can't live without each other and danced away into the night. But in reality, the whole combative thing might not be your best angle. They can make it work out in the movies, but in real life when all you do is disagree with her, it's very, very tiring. So avoid the Mr. Contrarian stuff unless you're Matthew McConaughey.

The thing to remember about romance is that it doesn't have to have a price tag on it. The most romantic things are cheap if not free. They just have to be cute and allow you to spend time with your crush. Of course, all romance is going to be "girly," so you can't think like a guy. Most girls aren't going to find it romantic to go to a monster truck pull or a tech fair. The Art of the Chase requires that you step outside of yourself and figure out what the object of your affection finds intriguing. Here are some starter ideas.

Nothing says "I really, really like you" like a guy willing to take a girl to a craft show.

Food

Events centered around food can be very romantic. And it doesn't have to be expensive food. In fact, most women love to cook with a man, so have her over for a night of fun and boiling water. If she's adventurous (i.e., not on a diet) then you can also do some food critic stuff. Pick one kind of food or one food item and decide to go to at least four different restaurants to taste test the same thing and compare. If you do this late at night, for example going to quirky all-night diners, you'll get extra points for romance.

Moonlit Walks

Walking is free, and for some reason women just love it. It's a chance to slow down and talk. Mmmm! Good stuff! So find a nice park or a romantic street to stroll down together.

Window-Shopping

Women love to shop, so add that to spending time with a hot guy and they have all they could ever want! But you don't have to spend money to make a shopping trip. Go furniture shopping and ask her what she would buy if she were furnishing a new house. Go to a cool part of town and look at houses—in fact, go on a Sunday when they have open houses and do some house tours. WARNING: Shopping is such a powerful thing in a woman's heart; combine that with the fantasy of a man who might someday buy her the things she's looking at—i.e., the perfect home—and you have a recipe for some strong romance. So please be cautious with this one. And women, if you are reading this, then please, please use your head. This is only pretend; he's not suggesting you two should sign up for the bridal registry and pick out your china. This is just for fun, but it can be a very powerful suggestion to your heart, so both of you need to be aware that this can really get a woman's mind racing. So guys, if you know this is just a temporary thing and you have no intention of a long-term relationship with her, then just avoid the window-shopping thing altogether. Guys who use this idea as a way to romance women and deceive them are the lowest of low. So with all of these hints, please don't use them for evil but use them for good, Luke Skywalker!

Dancing

Dancing is always a romantic thing for women. But if you don't want to pay a cover, try going to the park at night, rolling down all the car windows, playing some good slow-dancing music, and dancing under the stars. Nothing's more romantic than that!

The Art of Anticipation: The Strongest Ingredient for Romance

When it comes to romance, one of the best parts is the anticipation of an event. The longer a woman has to think about something romantic and wonderful happening, the

55

Adding newspaper to the fire of love is also very effective (and don't get me started about using lighter fluid . . . oh boy).

more excited she gets. The time to think gives her imagination time to grow. And women's imaginations are very powerful. They can really add kindling to the fire of love. That's one of the reasons we tell men to ask women out in advance of the event. It gives them time to dream, to prepare, to shop, to primp—all the things most women love to do. You can't imagine the things women can go through for a big romantic date. There's the pedicure and manicure extravaganza, the hairdresser, finding the perfect shoes to go with her new outfit. Then, of course, there's the hours of conversations with friends about the hoped-for event. All the prep is almost as fun as the actual date. Of course, this isn't the case for every single date or every single woman—we're all different, but for the most part women love anticipation. It's all part of the romance.

The Art of Chasing Girls

Hayley

I remember getting ready for the prom when I was in high school—of course that's the pinnacle of girlish fantasy—and planning ten hours for prep! Really. Four hours to lay out my clothes and go over them and over them. Time to take a long bath and do my nails, my hair, my makeup, etc. It all had to be meticulous! And I loved every minute of it. In fact, I had my mom *photograph* every minute of it. Dreamy! Of course, times have changed, and as I got older I got less, uh, weird, but I still love anticipating things. Dates with Michael, vacations with the family, parties with friends—I love the time it takes to get to the event. And most women do.

Michael

Yeah, I remember getting ready for the prom as well. I spent five minutes putting on my tux and one hour thinking up jokes that contained the word *cummerbund*.

Cummerbund—A broad waist sash, usually pleated, which is often worn with a tuxedo.

There are a few ways you as a man can allow a woman to live in that beautiful space of anticipation, and one of them is to give her plenty of notice for your date. That means you don't ask her out Thursday afternoon for Friday night. First, it's rather presumptuous, as if she isn't *already* booked! It also doesn't give her much time to live in anticipation. Now, we are talking about the early stages of the chase. After you've been dating for a while, plans and dates will become much more spontaneous. But in the early stages when you are wooing her, as they say, you have to give her some time to be wooed.

Anticipation is also a great gift to a woman when it comes to affection. Things like saying "I love you" and the first kiss are much more coveted and exciting when anticipation is allowed to build.

Hayley

I hate surprises. Maybe one of the reasons I hate surprises is because I love anticipating things. When someone gives me a surprise party or does something big and unexpected for me, it freaks me out. I need time to prepare my heart and mind for things. Maybe it's a weakness, but I want to know what's coming! Ah, anticipation is my friend! Some women are like me, and some just love surprises. If you want to do something for her without her knowing about it ahead of time, make sure she's a surprise-liking kind of girl. Otherwise, you may end up in a very uncomfortable situation.

Michael

And I love surprising people. Perfect fit, aren't we?! I remember trying to sleuth what style of engagement ring you liked best in hopes of surprising you. I had to learn to reprogram myself that you didn't want the surprise of the ring, but you wanted the anticipation of shopping for it and when (and if) I would pop the question. And I even had to fake an argument to throw you off the scent the day I asked you to marry me. You're a tough one to surprise!

The Art of Chasing Girls

The Women You Chase

Not all women are the same. In fact, you could probably argue that no two women are the same; that's what makes them such mysterious creatures. But you can often find a few common denominators when it comes to the women you chase. Certain personalities or life experiences can influence the way certain women react to your pursuit. Have a look and see if any of these generalities might apply to the woman you are after. If they do, you might find out some secrets to pleasing her heart.

The Independent Woman

If you have your eye on a successful, independent woman, there are a few things you need to know about chasing her. If she's used to being on her own and taking care of herself, it might look like she doesn't want you to take care of her. She can do it all herself, and she knows it. Doing it all on her own has become a habit. The problem a lot of guys have with this particular woman is that they don't go below the surface. They take her at face value, and they fail. Men have a desire to be needed, and this woman doesn't seem like she needs a man. That causes many a man to either steer clear of her or attempt the "just friends" angle in order to test the waters before going any further. In both cases, you end up missing out on the heart of this woman, and she completely overlooks you. In spending time with many a Ms. Independent, we have found out what she really seems to want but doesn't show: She wants a man who can manage her. She wants a man who shows himself to be more of a man than she is. That's really the challenge she secretly lays out before all men: Can you handle me? Are you stronger than me yet confident enough to allow me to be me? It sounds like a tough row to hoe, but for the brave man who is ready for an adventure, Ms. Independent is a breath of fresh air.

So, can you handle me?

If a man has a need to conquer, if he desires adventure and a challenge, then this is the woman who will give it to him. She is most often smart, confident, witty, and successful, or at least on her way to success. And because of all that, she can be a real handful, but that's where your love of a challenge comes in. Ms.

Independent doesn't need another "friend"; she needs a man.

So what does it mean to be a man to Ms. Independent? It means, in general, that you take charge of things. You aren't a dictator, but you know what the two of you are going to do and how you'll go about it. You aren't wishy-washy; you're certain. You aren't flying by the seat of your pants; you're in control. Even if you are spontaneous, you still seem to have things worked out ahead of time. Nothing takes you by surprise.

Ms. Independent often will test the men in her life to see if they truly can handle her. If you are aware of her tests, you are more likely to pass them when they come. Time and time again we hear independent women say things like, "Every time I get tough and try to take over or control him in some way, he lets me. I just wish I could find a guy who could stand up to me." Ms. Independent doesn't want a bully for a boyfriend; she just wants some-one who is strong enough not to cave to her bullying. That's the test. If you don't give in because she throws a fit or tries to wrestle control from you, then she's impressed. So with her you can't be playing up the nice guy routine and giving her everything she wants right when she wants it. That will instantly make you look like a pansy. A strong woman requires a strong man, so whatever you do, make sure not to be weak.

At the same time, she isn't going to take a man who "manhandles" her, if you will. She will appreciate a man who knows what he wants and won't cower at her power but who is also flexible enough to meet her where she is. Seem like a tightrope act? It kind of is, but then that's the kind of man Ms. Independent requires. If it seems like too much of a challenge for you, she might not be the one for you. The perfect man for Ms. Independent is one who knows who he is, what he wants, and how to get it. If you aren't secure in your manhood, she'll feminize you quickly. Just be prepared to hold on in loving firmness, and she'll love the woman you can allow her to be.

You're flexible. I'll give you that. But something about you strikes me as less than honest.

Hayley

I remember many years ago a pastor of mine telling me that I just needed a man who could handle me. At the time I didn't really know what that meant, but ten years and many failed relationships later, I finally figured it out. Michael was the only man I ever met who could handle me. He allowed me to be me, but he called me on stuff. He stepped up to the plate and took charge. He left me, a woman who usually felt like the man in a relationship, feeling like a soft, gentle woman. He was truly more man than me. And that allowed me to fall back into the femininity I had lost and revel in it.

Michael

I remember my mom wanted me to be a priest. Seriously.

But back on topic, for most of my dating years, I was the sensitive nice guy that turned into the frustrated "I should be leading but I don't know how" guy once in a relationship. I confused chivalry with sensitivity. Once I "got" that women don't need to marry their girlfriend, I started to finally become a man.

Many women have spent most of their lives being over-looked. They might not be as beautiful as most. They might not have the perfect body or the perfect life, but they have the perfect heart. The trouble is that not many men have taken the time to figure that out. This kind of woman, like all of us, loves the attention of a man. For her that attention instantly tells her that he is interested, because it's not an everyday occurrence. Because of that, she also might not believe your intentions at first. It will take you a little time to prove to her that you are true. She's interested not in a challenge but in a kind man who will find her beautiful and want to spend time with her. She doesn't necessarily crave witty repartee but will enjoy stimulating conversation. She more than likely will greatly enjoy grand gestures, because they mean she is on your mind. So send her flowers. Write her love notes. In general, unlike Ms. Independent, she will find your gentlemanliness very flattering. She isn't used to such things as men getting the door or carrying her bags, and she'll love it. It will truly mean a lot to her.

The difficulty with the shy girl is drawing her out enough to figure out if she's interested. Chasing her will require a bit more patience and attentiveness. Flirting might not go both ways at first, mainly because she's just too shy to attempt it or to believe that you are flirting with her. It's not part of her personality to be too gregarious, so you have to advance in a similar fashion. The shy girl is great for a man who isn't the life of the party himself. The old adage goes that opposites attract, and that might be true in some kind of weird fascination sort of way, but more often than not, opposites don't stick. There are, of course, exceptions, but for the most part, the more you have in common, the easier it is to click.

The Hot Woman

Beautiful women are being pursued by men almost continually. Everywhere they go, men stare and smile. They are never at a loss for attention. They know they can get almost any man they want, so what makes them choose you? The first thing you have to know about the hot woman is that she is taken aback by the man who *isn't* falling all over himself because of her beauty. She is shocked and even intrigued when you don't act like the other men around her. That doesn't mean you don't notice her beauty, because if you don't, she'll think you aren't interested, but it means that you notice it but don't belabor it.

66

The Art of Chasing Girls

The hot woman, like most men, needs to sense a little bit of mystery in her mate. She is so used to transparency that mystery really intrigues her. That means that you have to give her a little bit of attention at a time. You can't shower her with signs of affection, but you can't avoid affection either. A beautiful woman would love to be loved for her mind or her sense of humor as well as her beauty. So with her you have to click in those areas. You have to be strong enough to see past her exterior and delve into her heart. Unlike the shy woman or the neglected woman, grand gestures will more than likely be overkill to her. So show up to the door with a handful of wildflowers you picked on the way over rather than a dozen red roses. Don't buy her expensive gifts; make her something, but it can't look like you put too much effort into it. Your job is to be different from the rest of the guys who are pursuing her, and that generally means that you "get" her heart. You take the time and effort to look beyond her exterior, and you attempt to meet the needs of her heart. In general, avoid your first impulse to shower her

Ahhh. Tasteful yet simple, beautiful yet understated, inexpensive but not cheap. Now grab the flowers out of the vase and give them to her that way if there are no wildflowers on the way.

with compliments and gifts. That's been done! She wants something different, something deeper—unless she's still reveling in her own beauty, and in that case, a relationship with her will be fleeting.

With a beauty you almost have to be attentively disinterested. That means you let her know you like her, but you also act in such a way that she thinks you might not be interested. In other words, you give her a break from the continual attention she is used to and give her a bit more of a challenge to deal with. That will make you stand out and help assure her that you aren't just after her because you can't control yourself around her beauty. She yearns to be wanted for something deeper, and depth takes time. So even though for you it might be love at first sight, give her time to get there as well, and make sure that she is really, really into you before you confess your deep attraction. That way she'll be living on the edge of her seat in anticipation. It's like those TV shows where a man and woman have huge chemistry but season after season never get together. The tension that creates is exciting, even romantic. Rachel and Ross kept viewers in beautiful anticipation, and the hearts of women across America raced, just screaming for that final moment when they would fall into each other's arms and live happily ever after. Anticipation is a great way

The Art of Chasing Girls

to get the attention of the beautiful woman. All women love anticipating love, but the beautiful woman really needs it to get a connection.

The Super-Intelligent Woman

This woman will more than likely be turned on only by an intellect equal to if not superior to her own, so if you are just faking it, don't go after this one. She'll eventually see through you. It's hard for a really smart woman to respect a man who isn't as smart as her. She might be enamored with your rugged good looks, but over time your inability to understand her will leave her feeling empty. All women want to be understood, and this one is no different—it just takes a very special man to do that. So if you are up for the mental challenge, then this is the woman for you. She probably doesn't enjoy the grand gestures as much as the grand events. Things that will stimulate her mentally will draw you closer to her. Verbal sparring, cultural activities, and new experiences will be her biggest turn-ons.

What do you mean we can't use duct tape to fix your shoe? I thought you said you were smart?

Some women unfortunately haven't been treated well by the men in their lives. They are damaged. And that damage can play itself out in all kinds of ways. Some of them look for more men to abuse them; these are very dysfunctional women who need some healing before they are really ready for a relationship. They are the women who put themselves into belittling or menial roles in their careers and relationships. But other women who have been abused have simply shut down. They don't trust anyone. This kind of woman is closer to recovery than the former. But getting close to her will take work and lots of time. If you are interested in this woman, you have to be in it for the long haul. You also have to be man enough to maintain your masculinity without becoming another one of her girlfriends. You can't allow yourself to get hurt easily and to back away from her.

The Guy Who Chases

Women aren't all the same, and neither are the guys who chase them. So now it's time to check your chase mode, guys.

The Player

Once you're ready to get into the game, you have to be careful that you're not inviting too many women to play with you. When you do, you start to look like either a player or a loser, desperately trying every woman, hoping against hope that by upping the number of hits, you'll up your chances of success. You have to be strategic in your pursuit.

The Isolationist

If you love your job or you're just at your job most of your waking hours, it's no wonder you aren't meeting any women. If you spend most of your day playing video games in the room over your parents' garage, then surprise, surprise that you're alone and lonely. It's time to enter the world of the living instead of mashing buttons slaying the undead! If you're a workaholic, take a baby step and look for activities your workmates are involved in and join in. Coed softball or volleyball leagues, hiking trips, and movie nights—all of these things have been available to us in past jobs we've held. The great thing is you're doing things in a social setting but still can scratch that workaholic itch, since the activities are with your co-workers.

the least likely places to meet the woman of your dreams

in your cubicle
behind your Xbox 360
at Krispy Kreme
at a Star Trek convention (unless you dig Klingon chicks)

The Art of Chasing Girls

How to Ask a Woman Out

When asking a woman out on a date, consider the following ideas from *Marriable: Taking the Desperate Out of Dating*:

Ask her out for a specific event – Don't say, "Hey, we should go out sometime" or "You wanna do something?" Ask for what you want! "Would you like to go out to dinner next Friday night, say 7:00?" or "Hey, I've got two tickets to 'Scooby on Ice'—they turn the zamboni into the Mystery Machine. It's so cool!—would you like to go next Saturday?"

Don't ask her when a bunch of people are around – This is more for your protection than for hers. If she says no, you will have saved yourself a lot of embarrassment by not asking her in front of the entire office.

If she says no, don't ask why – Just say, "Okay, maybe another time," and walk away. If she wants to go out with you, she will give you another date that works, or she may just start flirting with you more.

Never ask her more than twice – If she says no two times in a row, she probably means no forever, unless she also tells you that she "would *love* to but can't this weekend, so how about next weekend?" You don't want to be a pseudo-stalker, but you also need to make sure she isn't just really busy. That's always a possibility.

Ask her yourself – Don't ask your friend to find out if she will date you. What is this, middle school?

Ask her out for one date at a time – Don't get greedy and ask her out for several dates at once. Women like a bit of mystery in their men. When you are all over her too soon, it's a real turn-off.

Be direct – Say, "Would you like to . . . ?" Avoid things like, "I know you are busy, but I was wondering if maybe one day you might wanna . . ." Get to the point and get to it fast. Don't be a wimp. Know what you want and be direct.

The Art of
Catching Mr. Right

3

In the words of the Seinfeldian philosopher George Costanza, "Always leave 'em wanting more!" Catching men is more like catching a little birdy or a bass than pouncing on a gazelle or a bunny rabbit. While men chase, women, in general, run. That is, they are the ones being pursued. But it isn't just running aimlessly, hoping a man will catch your scent and follow in hot pursuit; it's an art of its own. Catching a man isn't a passive activity; it requires forethought, wisdom, and patience. (Believe me, patience! It took me thirty-seven years to land one!) Okay, back to our analogy. Think of a beautiful bird that just flew in out of nowhere and landed on your deck railing. Surely you've lived long enough to know that you don't just run over to it, arms flapping in the air, saying, "Pretty birdy, pretty birdy!" and expect it to stay anywhere near you. In fact, if you do that, it might never come back. Same for men. You can't find Mr. Perfect and run up to him hoping to wrap your fingers around him, take him home, and have him sit on your shoulder the rest of his life. Okay, the analogy runs out there, sorry. But you get the picture. You'd scare the poor thing off if you ran up to it. So what can you do? How do you get a bird to stay or a guy to follow you home?

Polly want a remote control.

It's all in the way you chase. Men do the pursuing, the following, the asking, the seeking, but the woman's part of the chase is just as important. Women entice and attract the man they are interested in. This part of the chase can be the hardest part, because it's a more delicate movement. It requires precision, patience (there's that word again), and skill. And a woman is perfectly made for it. Your beauty makes that clear. Unlike in the animal world where the males are the most beautiful and vie for the female's attention, the form of the woman is by far more alluring than that of the man. But it isn't just about looks. Your personality, sense of humor, location, and approachability all play a part in the Art of the Chase.

77

Vocabulary Words

When it comes to the Art of the Chase, what women do is different from what men do in several ways. Here are some action words that best describe how women chase men:

entice: to attract artfully or adroitly or by arousing hope or desire

lure: to draw with a hint of pleasure or gain

allure: to entice by charm or attraction

attract: to draw by appeal to natural or excited interest, emotion, or aesthetic sense

And here are some action words that best describe how men chase women:

chase: to follow regularly or persistently with the intention of attracting or alluring

pursue: to find or employ measures to obtain or accomplish

woo: to gain the love or seek the support of another

win: to gain the support or favor of someone by action or persuasion

Equal Rights Equals Disaster

Equal rights have their place. Women should be paid the same salary for the same work. They should be able to vote, to buy land, to build businesses. Hurrah for equal rights—but not when it comes to the Art of the Chase. If you want equal rights when it comes to dating, then you're in for a rude awakening.

Think of it like this: Let's say you're ten again and you're playing with a bunch of your friends. You all decide to play chase and you pick who's "it." Then they close their eyes and you all run. Once he gets to ten, he opens his eyes and starts running after all your giggling, running-around friends. But you, O wise girl that you are, decide that you'll chase after him. So he spots you, your eyes light up, his eyes light up. He's coming in for the capture when suddenly you start running toward him. At first he might be excited and say something like, "What an idiot. Why is she running toward me? This is too easy." And **bam!** You run right into each other, and he's caught you. Game over. Everyone would look at you like "What a dork. That's not how you play chase!" Chasing requires one person to chase and the other to run away from, not run toward. Seems pretty rudimentary, but fast-forward that to your dating life.

If you think women can and should do the chasing, then more than likely that means you're chasing and the men are running—away from you! Not a real pretty picture.

But how would you like it if they did the chasing and you did the running for a change? Sound nice? It is. Men love to chase. Men love a challenge. They love to work at what they want, and in fact, if they don't have to work for something, they probably won't take very good care of it. Sound familiar? Women who do the chasing are seldom women who are well taken care of by their men. That's because they've set the precedent that they're the one in charge. The one leading. The one doing the taking care of. That's why you often hear them complain, "I'm tired of paying for everything" or "I'm tired of doing all the planning and all the work." The way it starts is the way it will end. So if you want to be pursued, if you want a man to be all over himself about you, if you want him to do the heavy lifting while you are cared for and doted over, then you've got to understand the Art of the Chase and how to catch men, starting with how to meet them.

Meeting Men

You don't have to sit by silently in the corner waiting for some man, any man, to come by and chase you. In the Art of the Chase, a woman's role is just as essential and just as active as the man's. You actually take the first step in the dance. Your job is, we might say, a more delicate one than his. It is to get his attention. That means to pique his interest, not to clobber him over the head and drag him home. You don't have to learn pickup lines or suffer from continual rejection like men do. You simply have to be you and, equally important, be available. No one ever caught a fish by wishing one would knock on the door, so why do we think Mr. Perfect will swim on by? Bass fishermen use lures to get the attention of the object of their attention. They fling the beautiful lure through the air till it lands delicately on the glassy water. Then they slowly pull it back to them, allowing it to glide through the water and send the hungry fish into a feeding frenzy. Catching men is like bass fishing. You don't jump out of the

Here fishy fishy.

boat and pounce on the fish; you lure them to you and then reel them in.

So what does it mean to be alluring? The definition of **allure** is "to attract artfully by arousing hope or desire using charm or attraction." But what does that mean in everyday life? Well, it means you figure out what your catch, men, find alluring or attractive, and you wave it in front of them so they'll follow after you. Not as if they're dull enough to follow anything that sparkles, but . . . oh, I guess they kind of are. Kidding! Some guys will follow anything in a skirt, but you probably aren't interested in those guys. So let's talk about how to be alluring to the good guys.

Location, Location, Location

They won't come knocking on your door, so if you want to fish, go where the fish are. That just means get out of the house, do things, have fun, and learn new stuff. Get out and get noticed.

Proximity

Once you've found a good location for dropping your lure, you're going to have to get close enough for them to see you. There are so many other fisherwomen around that proximity is key if you want them to notice you. Your first instinct might be to find a good one, sidle up to him, and ask him for his number, but remember, guys love the chase. And even though you might too, you have to think about chasing from a different perspective. You aren't hunting women, you're hunting men, and they require a different tact. You have to go after them while simultaneously making them think they are the ones chasing you. All most men ask is that you help them out by giving them some clear signals that you're interested. It's tough being the one to make the advances, because rejection hurts, but if you can help them to really get that you aren't going to reject them, then you're being a great help. So the first way to get their attention is by getting close. Close enough to look them in the eyes. Give 'em the four-second stare. It seems like an eternity when you're looking a total stranger in the eyes, but it's a great way for them to realize that you're there and not only that but you're interested. The good thing about it is that

Some men require something a bit more obvious.

The Art of Catching Mr. Right

it doesn't make you the pursuer; it just makes you look interested. And that's their signal to take things further.

Be Friendly

Once you've looked 'em in the eye, don't just stand there and wait for them to make the next move. Talk to them. Starting a simple conversation using the Art of Small Talk is a great way to not only meet a guy but also to make friends. If a guy isn't interested in you, he'll make his getaway quickly, and you can get on to greener pastures. Friendliness is a great flirting technique because you can be friendly with everyone. You can be just as friendly to the barista as you are to the hot guy looking at the magazine in the aisle next to you. It doesn't make you the aggressor, and it doesn't do any harm. So brush up on your small talk if you're feeling scared of this step. (Check out *The Art of Small Talk*, another *Marriable* book.)

If you've done these two things and the conversation has flowed well, then all you have left is to reel 'em in. Now, we are staunchly against women asking men out. It takes all the fun away from the guy and puts the woman to work. But that doesn't mean you can't still steer the conversation, gently helping the guy figure out that "closing the deal," as they say, is a sure thing. You can do this by continuing to make eye contact, touching his arm gently, and saying something confident like, "I've really enjoyed talking to you. I'm always up for a free cup of coffee!" or "It was great to meet you. You saved me from a boring night of boring guys." If he doesn't take the bait and ask you for your number, then it's not your lack of trying. He might just be spoken for, too shy to ask, or not interested. And if he's any of those three, you don't want him anyway.

I'd sing for you
if you'd just
reel me in.

What Men Love

This section could be really short—in fact, it could be just one word and that would pretty much sum it up. But then women would get all irate. "That's not true! Men don't all think about just one thing!" they'd scream. And we'd have to spend pages and pages proving why we were right. Funny thing is, if we said there's only one thing men really want and it's sex, most men would just smile and agree. In fact, in all our years and all our conversations on relationships, we've never found one man who would disagree. But since that just seems too preposterous for women to believe, we'll avoid saying that and move on to some things men like and, oh, by the way, hope will one day lead to the one thing they love—sex!

Okay, and maybe football.

The Art of Catching Mr. Right

The Mysterious Woman

If romance is a kind of aphrodisiac for women, then one could say that mystery is an aphrodisiac to men. Webster's dictionary says mystery "applies to what cannot be fully understood by human reason or less strictly to whatever resists or defies explanation." And though mystery often frustrates many a man, it is also what makes him love the woman who can't be fully understood. This is why when a woman talks too much, she loses her mystery. She gives him so much information that she no longer defies understanding. She wipes away the shroud of mystery that should encircle her and opens up the inner part of her being for the world to see. And the result is boring! But the mysterious woman arouses a man's interest. She makes him wonder what wonders lie inside of her. And in essence she weaves what might be considered the male counterpart to romance: a fantasy for the male psyche that she is the perfect woman.

Practicing mystery is a hard thing. Some women complain that it isn't being honest or that it's hypocritical. They complain that the man has to know them in order to love them, but the truth is that she has to be known in order to *feel* loved. She is bemoaning her own needs rather than being concerned with his. And the secret to true love is not an obsession with having our own needs met but a desire to meet the needs of another. The truly mysterious woman understands this, and she is willing to hide parts of herself in order to entice and excite the man in her life. She knows that he craves mystery like she craves romance, so she gives him what he yearns for. After all, isn't that the true definition of loving someone—giving them what they want, not what you want?

Mystery is a dying art. Most women find it unimaginable. They prefer the ease of letting it all hang out. They like themselves and want everyone else to as well. But we believe that if a woman can become truly selfless in the pursuit of her true love, then she can entice him much more adeptly than the selfish woman. Now, this doesn't mean that you forsake all of your needs and longings; it just means that you understand that in order to find what you long for the most—true love—you have to let go of the battle to please yourself and instead meet another human being halfway. We believe there are so many divorces in the world because people have bought the lie that their mate exists to make them happy, and so when that happiness ebbs, they feel they deserve something more. They abhor sacrificial love and instead opt for a me-centered

The Art of Catching Mr. Right

lifestyle. And that is a most unattractive quality in a person.

So what does a woman of mystery look like? How does she behave? And can you become a woman of mystery? The answer is yes, any woman can, and here is how.

Doesn't Dump

The mysterious woman never dumps her emotions or her feelings on a man. She is respectful of his feelings and understands that too much information means "bad date." Jealousy is a form of dumping, and it is very unattractive. Even if mysterious women feel a twinge of jealousy, they don't show it. They are confident in who they are and who is in control of their lives. They have no need for jealousy and don't dump their insecurities onto men.

Be careful of dumping off too much information.

Takes Her Time

When women rush, they lose their sensual appeal. A truly mysterious woman feels, or at least shows, no need to hurry. Not that she's late everywhere but rather that she has no need to rush the relationship. She doesn't have to know where the man stands on children right away. She doesn't involve him in her family life too quickly. She isn't anxious for anything; she is content in her life and calm about her future. When women pressure men, they lose their mystery. When they rush men emotionally, they lose their alluring appeal.

Shows Confidence

Confidence is very appealing to men—healthy men, anyway. And even if she doesn't feel confident, a mysterious woman can still display confidence by how she carries herself and dresses herself. Women who dress overly sexual show a big lack of confidence. Relying on your body to attract men is a big signal to bad men that you are a weak and damaged woman. A confident woman believes her body isn't a bargaining tool for men but is something to be revealed to one man in her life, her husband. That doesn't mean she dresses like a prude; she is stylish and well put together, but she is never vulgar or too revealing. Confident women don't show up with their excess baggage. And the men they go out with are relieved because of it. It is very alluring to find a woman who isn't damaged by another man. And even if you have been damaged, you can still act confident and not allow the damage that man has done to continue to ruin your life.

When a woman (or anyone, really) is confident, onlookers believe she must have something to be confident about. And that is very attractive. The mysterious woman is confident in her singleness, her personality, her relationships. She knows that she was created for the moment in which she lives. She isn't anxious to change. She isn't looking for salvation from a man. And though men love to fight for and protect women, they aren't looking for a hardship case who can't live without them. Inside each of us is a blueprint that points to something greater than a man, someone who is truly all we need, and therefore a man can never fill that need. When a woman trusts God, she is one of the most mysterious and beautiful things on the planet.

Confident women have a lot in common, and so if you want to look confident and therefore

This woman is extremely confident, and very mysterious.

91

mysterious, look no further than other confident women around you. When a woman is confident, she cares about the people she meets. Because of that, she learns their names. And if you watch, you'll observe that she will say their name back to them in conversation. Confident women ask questions of people to find out more about them because they care. The best conversationalists are people who focus on others instead of themselves. Confident women make others feel important; that's a very attractive quality. It's easy to spot an unconfident person; they are the ones who put all their focus on themselves. Their worries, their pains, even their successes. But confident women are just the opposite. So if you want to be a woman of mystery, watch other confident women and learn from them.

Now, let's see. I think he said his name was Rumplestilt something. Great, I can't remember.

Loves Life

A mysterious woman isn't a woman who is dark and depressed; she is a lover of life. She has a fire in her that is unavoidable. She has a passion for what she does and how she lives. When women complain and suffer in front of men, they look very unappealing. Men love women who love life; it gives them excitement. It makes them want to spend more time with you. So if you don't love life, then get to work. Find out what you love and do it. Bring passion to your life; throw out the bad thoughts and bring in the good ones. Love life and men will love you.

Is Honest with Herself

This is a big one in our book. After all, in **Marriable** we devoted an entire chapter to the subject "women lie to themselves to get what they want." So we know it's a hard instinct to break, but it has to be done if you want to become mysterious and, more importantly, to save yourself from the damage that lying to yourself can inflict. A mysterious woman isn't living in a dream world. She understands how guys think and doesn't project her feminine ideals and instincts onto them. She takes herself less seriously than the woman who lies to herself by believing that this guy is all she's ever wanted and if he leaves she'll never find another one again. Big lie! Big mistake. Guys can sense when you're making up a fantasy world around them, and it freaks them out. Being honest with yourself means you're not afraid of guys passing on you. You know you have weaknesses, and you aren't afraid of them or what they might do to guys' attraction to you. It's just another angle on confidence, really. Honesty says life is about more than this relationship and I'm not afraid of reality, nor do I intend to hide from it.

Can Be Charming

Charm is a very captivating characteristic, and the mysterious woman is full of it. It's hard to put your finger on what charm is, but we all know what it looks like when we see it. Charming people are focused on things outside of themselves. They seem more interested in what others have to say than in hearing themselves talk. They take a genuine interest in all people, even in those who can do nothing for them. They are easy to be with. They complain rarely, roll with the punches, laugh at life, and enjoy new experiences. Charming people are very easy to be with.

Some fortunate ones have a voice that can be one of the most charming things about them. If you have a beautiful accent or a deep voice, men will more easily find you charming. But even if you don't have a naturally unique or sensual voice, you can still work on not sounding like a screeching owl. Generally, talking softly is more charming than being a loud talker. No one wants everyone in the restaurant staring at them in dismay because their date is drowning out conversations three tables away. Take note of your voice, even ask your friends about it, and if it needs some tailoring, don't be afraid to work on it. It will greatly add to your charm.

10 Signs You Aren't Exactly Ms. Charming

1. You talk louder than everyone at the table
2. You frequently mispronounce words like "supposeably"
3. You use a toothpick after every meal, even on a date
4. You out-burp your date
5. You boss around the server
6. You are never satisfied, are picky, or complain a lot
7. You eat too fast or talk with your mouth full
8. You talk about yourself more than you listen
9. You find it hard to look people in the eyes
10. You wear so much perfume that people walking four feet behind you can still smell you

The Guys You Have Your Eye On

You can probably say in an instant the kind of guy you usually attract or go after. Most women tend to date the same kind of guy over and over again, and then they wonder why their relationships never work out. Not that we're saying that it's always the guy's fault, but a lot of the time if you keep dating the same kind of guy, you'll keep getting the same kind of heartache. Think about the guys in your past, or the lack thereof, and consider what kind of guy you are currently most attracted to. Although these are broad generalities, we think you might find some insight into the men that leave you wanting more or just leave you wondering why it never works out.

The Shy Guy

Lots of women think we aren't giving the shy guy a break. They say he needs some help. "He's just shy," they whine as their excuse for why they take control and ask him out. But just the fact that a guy is shy (1) doesn't mean that when he finds something he really wants he won't go after it and (b) doesn't mean that he can turn his masculinity over to you to run the relationship. Don't let shyness be an excuse for you to flip roles and start acting like a man. Because when you do, you upset the delicate balance of masculinity and femininity. And especially with the shy guy, you can become the leader, the one in charge, and that isn't an easy habit to break.

Now, a lot of women say they love being in control, so what's wrong with it? Not a lot at the beginning. But as the relationship drags on, a woman in that kind of position soon finds out what it's like to be the one making all the decisions and plans. She finds herself the one who is more with it, smarter, more driven, and better equipped to get things done, and suddenly she looks at her now boyfriend or husband with disdain because he can't seem to do anything as well as her. This quickly turns her guy into a henpecked man. When the woman is the one in control of most things in and around the relationship, nothing the man does is ever good enough for her, and so she begins to nag. In no time the man is feeling emasculated and neutered both! And his passion for his woman dwindles. The majority of men, and certainly the good ones, desire to be the provider, not the provided for. They desire to be the rescuer, not the rescued. They want to protect you, not be protected. All the things that a man is intrinsically good at are stripped away from him when women take control and run the relationship, and it often starts with the first move being made by the woman. The moral of the story is, don't take charge of the relationship. If you feel a need to be in control, control it in the beautiful way of using your femininity. Allure him, entice him, lead him to your heart. But don't pounce on him, snipe him, drag him, or hit him over the head. Leave that for the ignorant woman who thinks she can have her cake and eat it too.

When dating a shy guy, resist being a liberated cavewoman.

If you are still interested in the shy guy, here are some things to consider in the future. If you agree not to take over and overtake him, then you have to come up with a better plan for piquing his interest. The shy guy isn't always uninterested; sometimes he just doesn't have a clue that you would even like him. So with certifiably shy guys, you have to make it very, very clear that you wouldn't say no if he asked you. That means pulling out some heavy-duty flirting. Try eye contact and soft touching of his arm, leg, and so on when appropriate. Be near him whenever you can be, but most importantly, make it very clear that you'd like to go out with him. Ask him what he likes to do for fun, and if it sounds interesting let him know you'd love to do it sometime. Spend time getting to know him. The more you can draw him out of his shell, the easier it will be for him to maybe work up the nerve to ask you out. But beware, because this can easily become a "just friends" relationship, and then you'll have invested a whole lot of time in a guy who will never ultimately want to date you. You have to be honest with yourself and determine whether there might be any chance whatsoever with you two. If he's dating anyone else at all, even just one date, then chances are you will always be "just friends." If he never, ever dates, then it might be true that he's just too shy. But really give some thought as to whether or not you want a guy who can't pull the trigger to be the leader in your relationship. It can be agony, especially if you're a take-charge kind of girl.

The Bad Boy

A lot of women say they can't help it, they just prefer the bad boy. There are a lot of psychological reasons for that, but that doesn't mean that the bad boy will ever be the man you want him to be. Bad boys can be very appealing because of their generally strong sense of the masculine.

They aren't feminized, they don't throw themselves all over you, and they are mysterious, dangerous, and exciting. But the bad boy loses his appeal once you want to go beyond danger and into genuine love and affection. The bad boy is too selfish to love you unconditionally. If you find yourself drawn to the bad boy, take a serious look at what it is about him you love. Then see if you can't combine that with what you truly need—love, affection, commitment—in a good man.

The Big Kid

Some women find themselves strangely attracted to men who never really grow up. "He's just a big kid," they say. This is the guy who maybe still lives at home, spends hours and hours on his Xbox or GameCube, and loves the freedom of never really growing up. He probably makes you laugh and makes you cry. His inability to grow up is refreshing but also painful because you are forever the adult in the group. If you're attracted to guys who still act like kids, then maybe you aren't ready for a real relationship. You might not want to leave your childhood either, and that's okay for now. But once you want a real relationship that could really go somewhere, you might want to find a

Hayley

Growing up I was often attracted to the bad boy, and looking back, I can say that it was for two different reasons. One was that I wasn't interested in commitment. I liked being single, and I knew that the bad boy would probably ensure that I stay that way. So he helped me live in my dysfunctional bubble. But the second reason was that there was a hint of a challenge there that I loved. My challenge was to change him. I think most of us women have that crazy bone—we love to redo things like rooms and wardrobes and men. Trouble is, as I can testify, that never really works out. Bad boys don't change until they decide to change. And women who spend their energy trying to make them change only end up damaged in the end. What I really needed was a good man who understood the good parts of the bad boy but had the good qualities of the nice guy as well. When you find a good man, you will be attracted to his masculinity and impressed by his authenticity as well. The best combination, in my opinion, is the truly spiritual man who is deeply aware of and fond of his masculinity. That is the definition of a truly good man!

Michael

I had a brief bad boy period that was disastrous! Don't get me wrong, I got the girls and had the image, I just couldn't get over the guilt as a former nice guy. Fortunately for me (and you?) you met me after both of those parts of me got balanced out to a "good guy."

The Art of Catching Mr. Right

grown-up. The trouble with settling down with the big kid is that you often become a substitute for his mother. You'll find yourself picking up after him, nagging him, begging him to grow up. What you once found cute and playful will eventually become a pain in the butt when all you need is someone to make some grown-up decisions and pull some grown-up weight.

If you just can't give up the love of a big kid, then here are some things to consider. If what we've said about the man being the leader in the relationship ever applies, it *really* applies to the big kid. Taking over and chasing him only feeds his childish bone and gives him one more part of his life that he isn't in charge of. Helping the big kid to grow up is the best way to get his true love. So step back, get a life, and make him do the work. If he can learn to do the work now, he'll be a much better man in the long run.

Hey, baby! How about a date?

Mr. Successful

This guy seems perfect. He has a great job. He's making a good living, building a future for himself and his someday family. Not only is he acquainted with his masculinity but he's using it. He knows how to get what he wants in business and in love. He's the whole package. If that's who you're interested in, then what we've said about letting him lead really makes sense. But it doesn't mean he wants a pushover. Successful men like successful women. That doesn't mean you have to be a high-powered exec; it just means you have to be successful in life. Happy, carefree, kind, generous, all the things a woman of mystery is. Mr. Successful won't be turned on by a bashful, skittish woman. He will more than likely be looking for a woman he can talk with, play with, and work at chasing. His success signals that he likes a challenge, so a challenge you must be. Don't accept his spur-of-the-moment dates; be busy, because that means you're in demand. Don't be overly impressed with the things he does for you. Be grateful, but don't gush over his achievements or actions. When you are kind and sweet but not overly impressed, Mr. Successful just wants to try harder to impress you. In work, in life, and in dating, he wants what others haven't been able to get. So if you have ever been alluring or mysterious, you'll want to be with Mr. Successful. Remember that this guy loves a challenge, so be sure to give him what he wants: a real challenge!

This guy can be very attractive to women because of the challenge. Like men, women like a degree of challenge. That's why if you like this guy, you probably aren't a big fan of the "nice guy." Like the bad boy, the commitment-o-phobe is unattainable. The trouble with that is that you're fighting a losing battle. If he drops hints to you about his fear of commitment, take them at face value. Don't think that he's saying that in order to prove to you that you're much more special than the rest of womankind because he's going to commit to you. Nope, he's probably just letting you know that he's planning on breaking up with you eventually because marriage isn't in his future.

You won't marry me!? Are you seeing someone else?

When it comes to this guy, the same rules apply as to the rest, only even more so: You cannot chase this guy. His sole goal is not to be caught, so chasing him is an instant red flag to him. And he says to himself yet again, "I will not be caught." That's why catching this guy requires strict adherence to the Art of the Chase, female style. You have to let him do the chasing, and we mean the chasing the entire time. If you ever feel him start to lose interest, you have to back off, because you might just be smothering him. Let him feel the chase for the entire relationship. That's the only way you'll ever stand even the slightest chance of breaking his commitment fears. And we don't suggest trying. It isn't always the easiest thing to do. But if you can't resist this guy, then at least resist the temptation to let him know that. Be busy. Be commitment-o-phobic yourself, at least as far as he is concerned. Never, never ask the commitment-o-phobic guy his intentions. Never ask him when he's going to ask you to marry him. Never pressure this one or you'll lose him for sure.

Are you catching a pattern here? Standing back and letting the man do all the chasing is always, always the best way to catch a man!

Romance Warning

As we told the men, one of the definitions of *romance* in Webster's dictionary is "something that lacks basis in fact." And that seems like a pretty good definition. Romance is temporary. It isn't a way of life. And guys understand that;

it's women who have a hard time connecting the dots here. That's why manipulative guys can use romance to their advantage. They know you can't resist its pull and that the physical rush that you get from it—the high, if you will—is often confused with love.

Face it, women have a hard time separating how our hearts feel and being in love. In fact, you might be saying, "What's the difference?" It's simple, really: Love isn't a feeling. I know all the chick flicks tell you it is. And that feeling you get in your heart or the pit of your stomach sure feels like it must be love, but it isn't. Love is an action. If it were a feeling, then it couldn't be a commandment, because no one, not even God, can command you to feel. Therefore, love has to be an action. The trouble with love comes when a woman thinks that romantic feeling equals love and then runs into a guy who knows that about women (thanks to reading this book—oops!).

It's a continual dilemma: Women want romance from men. They crave it. But in order for them to get it, most often men need to be

Oh, my dove, you are a jewel among the fowl, you soar in the heights, leaving your mark on men's hearts (and heads). You have captured my attention ever since you entered my sights. How I love you.

107

told how to give it. It doesn't come naturally to them. So in an effort to help you out, we're teaching men some things that you find romantic. Now, buyer beware! When a guy gives you what you want—romance—don't be surprised if he's just using it to get what *he* wants—sex. That's the way the trade works: each bringing to the table what they have in order to get what they want. Not that we are condoning premarital sex; we think its stupid! But we've saved that for another book (check out ***Marriable: Taking the Desperate Out of Dating*** for more on the "if you loved me, you would" lie). We think it's just as dangerous to be romantic in a non-serious relationship as it is to be sexual, because romance is what turns women on. And being turned on plays with your mind. It tells you all kinds of lies and gets you to believe all kinds of things. The danger comes because some men will use romance to manipulate women and get them to feel more than is there, i.e., to lie to themselves about love. But since we can't stop men from using romance, we figure it's best to arm you with the truth. You have to be

I'm starting to get that mushy feeling inside. I wonder if I'm in love?

The Art of Catching Mr. Right

smart. You have to take time to get to know the guy and not translate that mushy feeling as true love. Be skeptical until you have all the facts. That doesn't mean you can't have fun and enjoy the moment; just be smart and don't lie to yourself about how amazing he is because your time together is romantic.

When you're dating a guy, you can often live with the illusion that the dreamy romance of today will be the dreamy romance of the rest of the relationship, and that just can't happen. Men can't be expected to keep up the romantic pace throughout the entire relationship. The reality is that life has its romantic moments and its mundane ones, and both have value. The trouble comes when women let their hearts rule their minds and start to believe that the romantic feelings they have translate into eternal love. That's not always the case. You can have romance without love. So our warning for the men is to be kind and not use romance to lead a woman on. You both need to know that the romantic moments you share have a powerful impact on your heart and cause you to see things differently than in your saner moments. There's nothing wrong with romance as long as both of you understand that it's going to ebb and flow and that it most certainly doesn't equal love. Love is a decision, not a feeling. Remember that, girls! Don't let the romance convince you of anything.

Shut Up and Be Mysterious

Once you've gotten a bite and you've moved on to date time, there's one important thing most women fail to learn, and that is to shut up! If you talk a lot, this statement probably has you pretty heated right now, but just hang on a minute. We aren't telling you never to say a word; we're just saying cut back a little. Too much information is never a good thing. Here's the deal: You might have so much to talk about—your pets, your mom, your job, your passions, your dreams, your hopes, your pains, your allergies—but what makes you think that he wants the 411 on all that makes you tick on the first date? A lot of women drown their dates in information. A guy is looking for a nice time with a woman. He wants to get to know her, to be enticed by her, to be intrigued, and all he gets is the Encyclopedia All-about-Me-ica on CD. Boring! So if you're a talker (**and there's nothing wrong with that**), you might want to just eliminate a few topics of conversation from your list. If some things are off-limits, then you won't run the risk of pouring cold water on the spark that got you two together in the first place.

So here's your new shut up list. These topics are off-limits, at least until he's pledged his love for you:

your food allergies

the cute thing your cat did last night

your ex-boyfriend

your menstrual cycle and anything that it might do to
your mind or body

You might be moaning, "But how will he get to know me if I don't talk about myself?" Okay, fair question. He won't, but no one expects to get to know another person in one or even two dates. Getting to know someone takes time, and dropping all your info on him on the first date just assures that you won't get any more time to get to know him. Too much information is one of the first things men say drives them off. In many instances "There was just no spark" means "There might have been a spark, but who could see it under the mound of information that she was shoving down my throat?"

Remember our analogy about how catching a man is like catching a bird? You don't want to run after him or

111

he'll fly away. Well, think about this. To get a bird to come to you, you feed him crumbs placed far away from you to start with, then gradually move them closer to you. Right? He follows the path, picking up each tasty morsel as he moves closer and closer. Now think of those small bread crumbs as information about you. What happens if you open up your bag and just dump the bread crumbs into a big pile all at once? You think the birdy is going to follow you in pursuit of more tasty tidbits? Or will he just get full on the major pile you dumped and waddle off to his nest? Too much information never got a man to follow after a woman. So slow down and be strategic. Give him just a few crumbs at a time and he'll be coming back for more.

With this in mind, consider the following list. Some things are fine to talk about; you just have to use all your faculties in order not to dwell too long on the topic or drown him in too many details. Some subjects can be broached but not belabored. This technique piques the curiosity and interest of your date enough to make him want more, and when that more isn't offered until a later date, that is called an incentive. Too much information offered at once is a disincentive. These things are not off-limits; they just have to be rationed. Think "bread crumbs."

your feelings

your hopes and dreams

your heartaches

your past

your family plans (how soon you want to marry, how many kids you want, etc.)

Feeeelings . . . whoa, whoa, whoa, feeeeelings . . .

Happily Ever After

It probably isn't a stretch to say every woman's dream is to live happily ever after. In fact, that's probably every man's dream as well, though he might not put it that way. And happily ever after can happen, to some extent—maybe it should be "happily most of the time after" to be more realistic, but we digress. The trouble with happily ever after comes not in the "after" part but in the "right now" part. We can have a tendency to put all our hopes for happiness into our current crush, but the problem with that is the pressure it can create on both you and him. The best thing to do when dating is to focus not on where you hope the relationship will go but on learning more about him and having a nice time today. When women start to get all futuristic on men, they can scare them off. And it doesn't have to be any words you speak; it might just be in the way you carry yourself or the loud ticking of the clock in your jeans. Either way, it's best to do what you can to concentrate on today, and tomorrow will take care of itself. It has enough worries of its own, as the saying goes. So slow the boat down. Shut your mouth a little. Listen a lot and enjoy the moment for what it is: a great time to get to know another human being and to learn to care for him.